HOW TO MAKE A GIRL FALL IN LOVE WITH YOU !

BE THE ONE

MYSTIC GURU

Made with ♥ on the Notion Press Platform
www.notionpress.com

Falling in love is a beautiful and complex experience that can bring immense joy and fulfillment to one's life. As a young boy, it can be difficult to navigate the intricacies of romantic relationships and understand what it truly means to fall in love. That is why I dedicate this book to all the boys who want to fall in love, in the hopes that it will provide guidance and insight on the journey towards finding and nurturing a meaningful and healthy romantic relationship.

First and foremost, it is important to understand that falling in love is not something that can be forced or controlled. Attraction and love are personal experiences that are influenced by a variety of factors and can take time to develop. Rather than focusing on trying to make someone fall in love with you, focus on being the best version of yourself and being a kind and respectful person. Show genuine interest in others, be a good listener, and communicate effectively. These qualities will make you an attractive and desirable partner to anyone.

It is also important to understand that love comes in many forms and can be expressed in a variety of ways. Romantic love is just one type of love, and it is important to also nurture friendships and familial relationships. As you grow and develop, you may also find yourself falling in love with people in different ways, such as through shared interests or a deep sense of connection.

One important aspect of falling in love is learning how to communicate effectively with your partner. This means being open and honest about your feelings, being a good listener, and respecting your partner's needs and boundaries. It also means being willing to compromise and work through any conflicts or challenges that may arise in the relationship.

Finally, it is important to remember that love is not a one-time event, but a continuous process that requires effort and dedication to maintain. A healthy relationship requires commitment, compromise, and a willingness to grow and evolve together.

In conclusion, I dedicate this book to all the boys who want to fall in love, in the hopes that it will provide guidance and insight on the journey towards finding and nurturing a meaningful and healthy romantic relationship. Remember that love is not something that can be forced or controlled, but rather, it is a personal experience that takes time and effort to develop and maintain. Be true to yourself, be kind and respectful, and always strive to be the best version of yourself.

Contents

Contents

Contents

Foreword

As the author of this book, I am honored to write this foreword and dedicate it to all the boys who want to fall in love. This book is a comprehensive guide to understanding the complexities of romantic relationships and learning how to navigate the journey towards finding and nurturing a meaningful and healthy love.

Falling in love can be a beautiful and transformative experience, but it can also be confusing and challenging. It is important to remember that attraction and love are personal experiences that are influenced by a variety of factors, and cannot be forced or controlled. This book is designed to provide boys with the tools and knowledge they need to navigate the complexities of romantic relationships and understand what it truly means to fall in love.

In this book, readers will learn about the different types of love, the importance of communication and understanding in a relationship, and the importance of being true to oneself in order to attract and maintain a healthy relationship. The book also provides practical tips and advice on how to navigate the dating world and develop the confidence and self-awareness needed to find and keep love.

I believe that this book will be an invaluable resource for boys who want to fall in love, providing them with the guidance and support they need to navigate this complex and rewarding journey. I hope that it will serve as a reminder that love is not something that can be forced or controlled, but rather, it is a personal experience that takes time and effort to develop and maintain.

Thank you for considering this book and I hope it will be useful and informative in your journey of falling in love.

CHAPTER ONE

INTRODUCTION

Falling in love is one of the most wonderful experiences a person can have. It brings joy, happiness, and a sense of fulfillment that can last a lifetime. However, the process of falling in love is not always easy or straightforward. For many boys, the thought of approaching a girl they are interested in and trying to win her heart can be intimidating and overwhelming.

The good news is that there are many ways to make a girl fall in love with you. From being confident in yourself and your abilities to being genuine and authentic, the key to success is to understand what girls are looking for in a romantic partner and to be the best version of yourself.

In this book, we aim to provide boys with practical and actionable advice on how to make a girl fall in love with them. We will cover a wide range of topics, including the importance of being respectful and considerate of her feelings, the value of being a good listener and showing that you care about what she has to say, and the significance of being ambitious and having goals in life.

We will also delve into more specific topics such as how to make a girl laugh, how to make her feel special, and how to build a strong and lasting connection with her. We will provide real-life examples and case studies to help illustrate the concepts discussed in the book and to make the advice more relatable and applicable.

In addition to providing practical advice, this book will also help boys to develop a deeper understanding of what girls are looking for in a romantic partner. We will explore the various factors that influence a girl's attraction to a boy, including personality traits, physical appearance, and life experiences. We will also discuss the importance of understanding and respecting her values, beliefs, and interests, and how this can help to build a strong and lasting connection.

The book is written in an easy-to-understand and conversational style, making it accessible to boys of all ages and backgrounds. Whether you are a teenager just starting to navigate the world of dating or an adult who is looking to improve your skills in attracting and falling in love with a girl, this book has something for everyone.

In conclusion, this book is a comprehensive guide for boys who want to make a girl fall in love with them. It is designed to help you understand what girls are looking for in a romantic partner, and to provide you with the knowledge and skills you need to build a strong and lasting connection. So, if you are ready to take your love life to the next level, let's dive in!

CHAPTER TWO

Confident in yourself and your abilities.

Confidence is a key factor in attracting a girl and falling in love. When you believe in yourself and your abilities, you exude a certain energy and charisma that can be very attractive to others.

However, it is important to note that confidence is not about being arrogant or boastful, but rather about being comfortable in your own skin and knowing your own worth. It is about having the courage to be yourself, even if that means being vulnerable at times.

Being confident in yourself also means being comfortable with your own flaws and imperfections. Everyone has them, and it is important to understand that they do not define you as a person. Instead, focus on your strengths and what makes you unique.

Additionally, having confidence in your abilities means being proactive in pursuing your goals and working towards your aspirations. It shows that you are driven and ambitious, which can be very attractive to a girl.

In short, when you are confident in yourself and your abilities, you exude a sense of self-assurance and security that can be very attractive to a girl. It allows you to be yourself and pursue your goals with conviction, which can be the foundation of a strong and lasting relationship. Remember that confidence is not something that can be faked, it is something that is built through self-awareness, self-acceptance and self-love.

CHAPTER THREE

GENUINE AND AUTHENTIC, DON'T TRY TO BE SOMEONE YOU'RE NOT.

When trying to attract a girl and fall in love, it can be tempting to try and be someone you're not in order to impress her. However, it is important to remember that being genuine and authentic is crucial in building a strong and lasting relationship.

When you try to be someone you're not, you risk putting on a facade that will eventually crumble. It is not sustainable in the long run and will only lead to disappointment and dissatisfaction for both parties. Instead, it's much better to be true to yourself and let your unique qualities shine through.

Being genuine also means being honest and upfront about your feelings and intentions. If you're not sure about your feelings for her, it's better to be honest and let her know, rather than leading her on. Authenticity is also about being true to your own values and beliefs, and not compromising them just to impress a girl.

Additionally, when you are genuine and authentic, you are more likely to attract a girl who is also genuine and authentic. This is because you both can be yourselves around each other, which leads to a more comfortable and relaxed dynamic and a deeper emotional connection.

In short, when trying to attract a girl and fall in love, it is important to be genuine and authentic. Don't try to be someone you're not, as it will only lead to disappointment in the long run. Instead, be true to yourself, be honest, and let your unique qualities shine through. This is the foundation of a strong and lasting relationship.

CHAPTER FOUR

Interest in Getting to Know Her and Actively Listen to Her

One of the most important things a boy can do to attract a girl and fall in love is to show interest in getting to know her and actively listen to her. This means taking the time to ask her questions and truly listen to her answers, rather than just waiting for your turn to speak.

Active listening involves paying attention not only to her words, but also to her body language, tone of voice, and facial expressions. It is about understanding her perspective and showing empathy towards her feelings. It also means acknowledging and validating her thoughts and opinions. When you actively listen to her, you are showing her that you care about her and that she matters to you.

Furthermore, showing interest in getting to know her means taking the time to learn about her interests, hobbies, and goals. It means making an effort to understand her as a person and to build a deeper connection with her.

Additionally, it's not just about listening, but also showing that you care about what she's saying and responding to it. Asking follow-up questions, giving feedback or relating to what she's saying are all ways to show that you're actively engaged in the conversation and interested in getting to know her.

In short, showing interest in getting to know her and actively listening to her is crucial in attracting a girl and falling in love. It demonstrates that you care about her and value her as a person. It allows you to build a deeper connection and understanding with her, which is the foundation of a strong and lasting relationship.

CHAPTER FIVE

AMBITIOUS AND HAVE GOALS IN LIFE.

Being ambitious and having goals in life is an important aspect of attracting a girl and falling in love. When a boy has ambition and a sense of purpose, it shows that he is driven and motivated, and that he is actively working towards creating a better future for himself and those around him.

Having goals in life also means being proactive in pursuing them, and working towards achieving them. This shows that you are a responsible and dependable person, who is capable of committing to something and seeing it through to the end. It also shows that you have a clear vision of what you want in life, and that you are willing to put in the effort to make it happen.

Furthermore, when you have goals in life, you are more likely to be fulfilled and satisfied with your life, which can make you a more attractive and interesting person to a girl. When you are content and happy with your life, it makes it easier for you to be a supportive and caring partner.

Additionally, having goals and working towards them can also be a shared interest that you can bond over. You can discuss your aspirations, offer each other support and encouragement, and even work together towards achieving them. This can strengthen the connection between you and her.

In short, being ambitious and having goals in life is an important aspect of attracting a girl and falling in love. It shows that you are driven and motivated, responsible and dependable, and that you have a clear vision for your future. It also creates opportunities for shared interests and bonding, which can be the foundation of a strong and lasting relationship.

CHAPTER SIX

RESPECTFUL AND CONSIDERATE OF HER FEELINGS.

Being respectful and considerate of a girl's feelings is crucial for attracting her and falling in love. Respect means treating her with dignity and courtesy, valuing her opinions and choices, and being sensitive to her needs and feelings.

Being considerate of her feelings means taking the time to understand how she feels about a situation, and being mindful of how your actions and words may affect her. It means being willing to compromise and put her needs before your own.

When a boy is respectful and considerate of a girl's feelings, it shows that he values her as a person and that he cares about her well-being. It also demonstrates that he is mature and emotionally intelligent, which are important qualities in a romantic partner.

Additionally, showing respect and consideration towards her feelings also means being honest and transparent with her. It means being open and willing to communicate your own feelings and thoughts in a way that is respectful and non-judgmental. It also means being willing to listen and understand her perspective, even when you disagree with her.

In short, being respectful and considerate of a girl's feelings is essential for attracting her and falling in love. It shows that you value her as a person and that you care about her well-being. It also demonstrates maturity and emotional intelligence, which are important qualities in a romantic partner. Additionally, it lays the foundation for open and honest communication, which is crucial for any healthy and lasting relationship.

CHAPTER SEVEN

LISTEN GOOD AND SHOW THAT YOU CARE ABOUT WHAT SHE HAS TO SAY.

Being a good listener and showing that you care about what a girl has to say are vital for attracting her and falling in love. Listening is a fundamental aspect of communication, and it is one of the most important ways to show someone that you care about them and value their thoughts and feelings.

When you actively listen to a girl, you demonstrate that you are interested in what she has to say and that you are willing to take the time to understand her perspective. It also shows that you respect her and value her opinions. This can make her feel heard and understood, which can be incredibly important in building trust and emotional connection.

Additionally, being a good listener also means being responsive and engaging in the conversation. This means asking questions, providing feedback, and showing that you are actively listening and paying attention to what she is saying. It also means avoiding interruptions and distractions, such as checking your phone or being preoccupied with other things, as it can make her feel unimportant.

In short, being a good listener and showing that you care about what a girl has to say are essential for attracting her and falling in love. It shows that you are interested in her and that you respect and value her opinions and feelings. It also lays the foundation for strong and healthy communication, which is crucial for any lasting relationship.

CHAPTER EIGHT

SUPPORT AND BELIEVE HER.

Being supportive and believing in a girl is crucial for attracting her and falling in love. Support means being there for her, both emotionally and physically, and being willing to help her when she needs it. It means being her cheerleader and believing in her abilities, even when she may doubt herself.

Believing in a girl means having faith in her and her capabilities. It means being convinced that she can achieve her goals and dreams and encouraging her to pursue them. It means being her rock, her confidant, and her biggest fan.

When a boy is supportive and believes in a girl, it shows that he cares about her and that he is invested in her success and happiness. It also demonstrates that he is trustworthy and dependable, which are important qualities in a romantic partner.

Additionally, being supportive and believing in her also means accepting her for who she is and not trying to change her. It means being non-judgmental and open-minded, and it means encouraging her to be true to herself.

In short, being supportive and believing in a girl is essential for attracting her and falling in love. It shows that you care about her and that you are invested in her success and happiness. It also demonstrates that you are trustworthy and dependable, which are important qualities in a romantic partner. Additionally, it lays the foundation for acceptance and understanding, which are crucial for any healthy and lasting relationship.

CHAPTER NINE

HONEST AND TRANSPARENT

Being honest and transparent in your intentions and actions is crucial for attracting a girl and falling in love. Honesty means being truthful and open in your communication and actions. It means being genuine and authentic, and not hiding your true feelings or intentions. Transparency, on the other hand, means being open and upfront about your actions, and not keeping secrets or being vague.

When you are honest and transparent in your intentions and actions, it shows a girl that you respect and value her. It demonstrates that you trust her and that you are willing to be vulnerable and open with her. It also lays the foundation for trust, which is essential for any healthy and lasting relationship.

Additionally, being honest and transparent also means being accountable for your actions. It means taking responsibility for your mistakes and being willing to apologize when necessary. It also means being consistent in your actions and words, and not making promises you can't keep.

In short, being honest and transparent in your intentions and actions is crucial for attracting a girl and falling in love. It shows that you respect and value her and that you are willing to be vulnerable and open with her. It lays the foundation for trust and accountability, which are essential for any healthy and lasting relationship. It also demonstrates your maturity and integrity, and that you are a reliable and trustworthy person.

CHAPTER TEN

BE PATIENT AND DON'T RUSH OR PRESSURE HER

Being patient and not rushing or pressuring a girl is crucial for attracting her and falling in love. Patience means being willing to take the time to get to know her and build a connection without expecting immediate results. It means not pushing her to move faster than she is comfortable with and not putting pressure on her to make a commitment before she is ready.

Rushing and pressuring a girl can make her feel uncomfortable and can push her away. It can make her feel like you are not interested in getting to know her and building a genuine connection, but rather that you are just looking for something casual or short-term. It can also make her feel like you are not respecting her boundaries and her need for space and time.

On the other hand, being patient and not rushing or pressuring her shows that you are genuinely interested in getting to know her and that you respect her needs and feelings. It demonstrates that you are willing to take the time to build a solid foundation for a healthy and long-lasting relationship. It also shows that you are someone who can be trusted and dependable in the long run.

In short, being patient and not rushing or pressuring a girl is essential for attracting her and falling in love. It shows that you respect her needs and feelings, and that you are genuinely interested in getting to know her and building a connection. It also demonstrates that you are someone who can be trusted and dependable in the long run, which are important qualities in a romantic partner.

CHAPTER ELEVEN

Sense of Humor and Can Make Her Laugh

Showing a girl that you have a sense of humor and can make her laugh is an important aspect of attracting her and falling in love. A sense of humor is often seen as a desirable trait in a romantic partner, as it can help to lighten the mood and make the relationship more enjoyable.

When you can make a girl laugh, it shows that you are confident, relaxed, and comfortable in your own skin. It also demonstrates that you are able to connect with her on an emotional level and that you are able to understand her perspective. Humor can also be a great way to break the ice and make her feel more at ease, which can be especially important in the early stages of a relationship.

However, it is important to remember that humor is subjective, and not everyone finds the same things funny. Therefore, it's important to be aware of the girl's sense of humor and try to make her laugh with things she find funny. Also, avoid making fun of her or anyone else in the process.

In addition to making her laugh, it is also important to show her that you can laugh at yourself and that you are able to take a joke. This can demonstrate that you are comfortable in your own skin and that you are not overly sensitive or defensive.

In short, showing a girl that you have a sense of humor and can make her laugh is an important aspect of attracting her and falling in love. It demonstrates that you are confident, relaxed, and comfortable in your own skin. It also shows that you are able to connect with her on an emotional level and that you are able to understand her perspective. But it is important to remember that humor is subjective and avoid making fun of her or anyone else.

CHAPTER TWELVE

EMOTIONAL INTELLIGENCE AND UNDERSTANDING OF HER EMOTIONS

Showing a girl your emotional intelligence and understanding of her emotions is crucial for attracting her and falling in love. Emotional intelligence is the ability to understand and manage one's own emotions, as well as the emotions of others. It is the key to healthy communication, relationships, and emotional well-being.

When you show a girl your emotional intelligence and understanding of her emotions, you demonstrate that you are aware of her feelings and that you are willing to work to understand them. It shows that you are empathetic and compassionate, and that you are able to put yourself in her shoes. This can be incredibly powerful in building trust and emotional connection.

Additionally, showing emotional intelligence and understanding of her emotions also means being able to manage your own emotions in a healthy and effective way. This means being able to regulate your feelings and express them in a constructive manner, rather than acting impulsively or lashing out. It also means being able to understand and accept her emotions, even when they may be different from your own.

In short, showing a girl your emotional intelligence and understanding of her emotions is essential for attracting her and falling in love. It demonstrates that you are aware of her feelings and that you are willing to work to understand them. It also shows that you are empathetic and compassionate, and that you are able to manage your own emotions in a healthy and effective way. All of these qualities are important in building trust and emotional connection in any relationship.

CHAPTER THIRTEEN

TRUSTWORTHY AND DEPENDABLE

Showing a girl that you are trustworthy and dependable is crucial for attracting her and falling in love. Trust and dependability are essential components of any healthy and lasting relationship, and they are key factors in building trust and emotional connection with a girl.

Being trustworthy means keeping your promises and being honest and transparent with her. It means being reliable and following through on what you say you will do. It also means being confident in yourself and your abilities and being responsible and accountable for your actions.

Being dependable means being there for her when she needs you, both emotionally and physically. It means being supportive and being willing to help her in times of need. It also means being a good listener and being present in the moment, rather than being preoccupied with other things.

When a boy shows a girl that he is trustworthy and dependable, it demonstrates that he is responsible and reliable, and it lays the foundation for trust and emotional connection. It also shows that he cares about her and that he is invested in the relationship.

Additionally, being trustworthy and dependable also means being respectful and considerate of her feelings. It means being honest and transparent in your communication and being willing to compromise and work through challenges together.

In short, showing a girl that you are trustworthy and dependable is essential for attracting her and falling in love. It demonstrates that you are responsible and reliable, and it lays the foundation for trust and emotional connection. It also shows that you care about her and that you are invested in the relationship, which are important qualities in a romantic partner.

CHAPTER FOURTEEN

GOOD COMMUNICATOR AND CAN EXPRESS YOURSELF EFFECTIVELY

Effective communication is a crucial component of any relationship, and it is especially important for attracting a girl and falling in love. Good communication skills involve being able to express yourself clearly and effectively, as well as being able to listen actively and respond appropriately.

When you show a girl that you are a good communicator, you demonstrate that you are confident and capable of expressing your thoughts and feelings. This can make her feel heard and understood, which is important for building trust and emotional connection. Additionally, being a good communicator also means being able to effectively manage conflicts and resolve differences, which are important skills in any relationship.

Furthermore, good communication also involves being able to express your needs and boundaries, as well as being able to listen to and respect hers. This means being honest and transparent in your communication, as well as being willing to compromise and work together to find mutually beneficial solutions.

In short, being a good communicator and showing that you can express yourself effectively is essential for attracting a girl and falling in love. It demonstrates that you are confident and capable, and it lays the foundation for strong and healthy communication, which is crucial for any lasting relationship.

CHAPTER FIFTEEN

Responsible and Reliable Person

Showing a girl that you are a responsible and reliable person is crucial for attracting her and falling in love. Responsibility and reliability are important traits that demonstrate maturity, stability, and dependability. They are qualities that are highly valued in a romantic partner, as they provide a sense of security and trust.

Being responsible means taking ownership of your actions and being accountable for your decisions. It means being dependable and following through on your commitments, whether they are big or small. It also means being proactive and taking the initiative to make things happen, rather than being passive and waiting for things to happen to you.

Being reliable means that you can be counted on and that you are there for your partner when they need you. It means being consistent in your actions and decisions, and it means being trustworthy and dependable. It also means being there for your partner emotionally, providing support and comfort when they need it.

When a boy shows a girl that he is a responsible and reliable person, it demonstrates that he is trustworthy and dependable, and that he is someone she can count on. It also shows that he is mature and stable, and that he is able to provide a sense of security and trust.

In short, showing a girl that you are a responsible and reliable person is essential for attracting her and falling in love. It demonstrates that you are trustworthy and dependable, and that you are someone she can count on. It also lays the foundation for stability and security, which are crucial for any healthy and lasting relationship.

CHAPTER SIXTEEN

OPEN-MINDED AND WILLING TO TRY NEW THINGS

Showing that you are open-minded and willing to try new things can be a powerful tool in attracting a girl and falling in love. Being open-minded means being receptive to new ideas, perspectives, and experiences, and it is a quality that is highly valued in a romantic partner.

Being open-minded can help you connect with a girl on a deeper level by showing that you are willing to understand and embrace her experiences, interests, and values. It also demonstrates that you are not closed off to new possibilities and that you are willing to explore new things together.

In addition to helping you connect with a girl, being open-minded can also make you a more interesting and engaging person. When you are willing to try new things, you can learn new skills, experience new cultures, and broaden your horizons. This can make you a more well-rounded and interesting person, which can be very attractive to a girl.

Moreover, being open-minded can also help you build trust and rapport with a girl. When you are willing to try new things, you demonstrate that you are willing to step outside of your comfort zone, and this can make her feel more comfortable and confident in your relationship.

So, what are some things that you can do to show a girl that you are open-minded and willing to try new things? There are many ways, but here are a few suggestions:

Try new foods: Step out of your comfort zone and try new cuisines or dishes that you have never tried before.

Take up a new hobby: Try something new that you have always been interested in, such as painting, photography, or rock climbing.

Explore new places: Take a road trip, visit a new city, or try a new activity, like skydiving.

Read new books or watch new movies: Expand your knowledge and understanding of different cultures and perspectives.

Be open to new experiences: Try new things that may be outside of your comfort zone, such as trying a new dance or sport.

In conclusion, showing that you are open-minded and willing to try new things can be a powerful tool in attracting a girl and falling in love. It demonstrates that you are receptive to new ideas, perspectives, and experiences, and it can help you build trust, rapport, and a deeper connection with a girl. So, be brave, be adventurous, and be open to new possibilities!

CHAPTER SEVENTEEN

PASSION AND PURPOSE IN LIFE

Showing a girl that you have a passion and purpose in life is key to attracting her and falling in love. When you have a clear direction and drive, it not only makes you a more interesting and engaging person, but it also shows that you are ambitious and confident. These qualities are extremely attractive to women and can be a huge factor in building a connection.

Having a passion means being enthusiastic about something and having a sense of purpose. It could be anything from a hobby, a career, or a cause that you are deeply invested in. When you have a passion, you radiate energy and excitement, which can be infectious and engaging for those around you.

In addition to being attractive, having a passion also demonstrates that you are proactive and driven. When you are pursuing something you are passionate about, you are showing that you are willing to work hard and put in the effort to achieve your goals. This shows that you have a strong work ethic and a desire to succeed, which are qualities that many women look for in a partner.

Having a purpose in life is equally important. It means having a sense of direction and knowing what you want to achieve. It also means being focused and motivated, and having a plan for how to get there. When you have a purpose, you are more confident and self-assured, and this can be very attractive to women.

Furthermore, having a passion and purpose in life can also bring you closer together. When you share a common interest or goal, it gives you a bond to build upon and a reason to support each other. This can create a deeper level of connection and a sense of shared purpose, which can be incredibly important in a relationship.

In conclusion, showing a girl that you have a passion and purpose in life is an important step in attracting her and falling in love. It demonstrates that you are interesting, ambitious, and confident, and it can help build a deeper connection between you. When you have a clear direction and drive, you become a more attractive and engaging person, which can be a huge factor in building a lasting relationship.

CHAPTER EIGHTEEN

Respectful of Her Boundaries and Needs

Respect is an integral part of any relationship, and showing respect for a girl's boundaries and needs is essential for attracting her and falling in love. Boundaries are important for everyone, and they are especially crucial in a romantic relationship. They provide a sense of safety and security, and they allow individuals to maintain their individuality and independence.

When a boy shows respect for a girl's boundaries and needs, he demonstrates that he cares about her and that he is willing to prioritize her feelings and well-being. This can make her feel valued and appreciated, and it can also help to build trust and emotional connection.

Respectful behavior includes asking for permission before initiating physical contact, such as holding hands or hugging. It also means being mindful of her personal space and not invading it without permission. It means respecting her privacy and not sharing information or secrets that she has confided in you without her consent.

Another aspect of respecting a girl's boundaries and needs is being mindful of her schedule and availability. If she has plans or commitments, it's important to be understanding and not pressure her into cancelling them. Additionally, it's important to respect her time and not monopolize it, and to be understanding if she needs time for herself or to recharge.

In short, showing respect for a girl's boundaries and needs is an essential component of attracting her and falling in love. It demonstrates that you care about her and that you are willing to prioritize her feelings and well-being. It also helps to build trust and emotional connection, which are crucial for any healthy and lasting relationship.

Finally, it is important to note that respecting a girl's boundaries and needs is a two-way street. Just as it's important for a boy to show respect, it's also important for a girl to do the same. Both parties need to be mindful of each other's feelings and well-being, and they need to be willing to compromise and work together to build a relationship based on mutual respect and understanding.

CHAPTER NINETEEN

RESPECT FOR YOURSELF AND YOUR OWN NEEDS

Showing that you have respect for yourself and your own needs is an important aspect of attracting and falling in love with a girl. When you have self-respect, you show that you value yourself and that you have high standards for how you want to be treated. This can make you more attractive and appealing to a potential partner because it demonstrates that you are confident and self-assured.

Having respect for your own needs means taking care of yourself and not sacrificing your own well-being to please others. It means setting boundaries and being honest about what you want and need in a relationship. When you have respect for your own needs, you are less likely to compromise your values or make sacrifices that are not in your best interest.

When a girl sees that you have respect for yourself and your own needs, she is more likely to respect you as well. She will understand that you are a person who values yourself and that you have high standards for how you want to be treated. This can make you more attractive to her because she will see that you are a person of integrity who is not willing to compromise your values or make sacrifices that are not in your best interest.

Having self-respect can also help to build trust and emotional connection in a relationship. When you have respect for yourself, you are more likely to communicate openly and honestly with your partner. You are also more likely to be a good listener and to show that you care about what she has to say. This can help to build trust and emotional connection because it demonstrates that you are interested in her and that you value her opinions and feelings.

Additionally, having self-respect can also help to create a more fulfilling and satisfying relationship. When you have respect for yourself, you are more likely to be happy and content with your life, which can make you a more attractive and appealing partner. You are also more likely to have a positive attitude and to approach your relationship with a sense of optimism, which can help to create a more fulfilling and satisfying relationship.

In conclusion, showing that you have respect for yourself and your own needs is essential for attracting and falling in love with a girl. It demonstrates that you are confident and self-assured, and it makes you more attractive and appealing to a potential partner. Additionally, it helps to build trust and emotional connection and creates a more fulfilling and satisfying relationship. By respecting yourself and your own needs, you are setting the stage for a healthy and lasting relationship

CHAPTER TWENTY

KIND AND COMPASSIONATE PERSON

Showing a girl that you are a kind and compassionate person is one of the most important things a boy can do if he wants to fall in love with her. Kindness and compassion are essential traits that make a person attractive, and they are also qualities that are highly valued in a romantic partner.

Kindness involves being considerate and understanding of others, and it means being willing to help and support those in need. It means being selfless and putting others before yourself, even when it may be inconvenient or uncomfortable. When a boy shows a girl that he is kind, it demonstrates that he cares about her and that he is invested in her happiness.

Compassion, on the other hand, involves being empathetic and understanding of others' feelings and experiences. It means being able to put yourself in someone else's shoes and understand their perspective. When a boy shows a girl that he is compassionate, it demonstrates that he is able to understand her emotions and that he is willing to support her through difficult times.

In addition to showing a girl that you are kind and compassionate, it is also important to consistently demonstrate these traits in your actions. This means being respectful and courteous, even when you may disagree with her. It also means being understanding and forgiving, and being willing to make compromises and sacrifices for the relationship.

Furthermore, being kind and compassionate also means being supportive and non-judgmental. It means accepting her for who she is and encouraging her to be true to herself. It means being patient and understanding, even when she may be going through difficult times.

In short, showing a girl that you are a kind and compassionate person is one of the most important things a boy can do if he wants to fall in love with her. Kindness and compassion are essential traits that make a person attractive, and they are also qualities that are highly valued in a romantic partner. Demonstrating these traits consistently and in your actions will demonstrate to her that you care about her and that you are invested in her happiness and well-being.

CHAPTER TWENTY-ONE

GOOD PROBLEM SOLVER AND CAN HANDLE CONFLICT EFFECTIVELY

Showing a girl that you are a good problem solver and can handle conflict effectively is essential for attracting her and falling in love. Relationships, like all things in life, come with their own set of challenges and difficulties. How a couple handles these challenges can make or break the relationship.

A good problem solver is someone who can identify the root cause of an issue, come up with a solution, and take action to resolve it. This shows that you are capable and competent, and that you are not afraid of tackling difficult situations. It also demonstrates that you are a responsible and dependable partner who is willing to take the lead when necessary.

Handling conflict effectively is equally important. Conflict is an inevitable part of any relationship, and how a couple handles it can have a significant impact on the health and longevity of the relationship. An effective conflict resolution requires good communication skills, the ability to listen and understand each other's perspective, and the willingness to compromise and find a mutually acceptable solution.

When a boy can demonstrate that he is a good problem solver and can handle conflict effectively, it shows that he is mature and responsible, and that he has the skills to navigate challenges and difficulties that may arise in the relationship. It also gives a girl the peace of mind and security that she needs to trust and rely on him.

Moreover, being a good problem solver and handling conflict effectively can also strengthen the bond between the couple. When a couple can work together to resolve challenges, they are more likely to feel connected and supported, and they are more likely to grow as individuals and as a couple.

In short, showing a girl that you are a good problem solver and can handle conflict effectively is essential for attracting her and falling in love. It demonstrates that you are mature and responsible, and that you have the skills to navigate challenges and difficulties that may arise in the relationship. It also gives her the peace of mind and security she needs to trust and rely on you, and it strengthens the bond between the couple.

CHAPTER TWENTY-TWO

Team Player and Can Work Well in a Relationship

Showing a girl that you are a good team player and can work well in a relationship is an important aspect of attracting her and falling in love. In a relationship, it is essential to be able to work together as a team, communicate effectively, and support each other.

A good team player is someone who is cooperative, flexible, and willing to work together to achieve common goals. In a relationship, this means being willing to compromise, listen to each other's perspectives, and work together to resolve conflicts. It also means being there for each other, supporting each other, and helping each other to achieve personal and shared goals.

Being a good team player also requires effective communication. In a relationship, it is important to be able to express your thoughts and feelings in a clear and concise manner, and to be willing to listen to your partner's perspective. It also means being open and honest with each other, and being willing to work together to find solutions to problems.

In addition, being a good team player also means being supportive of your partner's goals and aspirations. Whether it's supporting her dreams of pursuing a career, traveling the world, or starting a family, it is important to be her biggest cheerleader and to believe in her. This type of support not only strengthens the relationship, but it also shows that you care about her and that you are committed to helping her achieve her goals.

Finally, being a good team player also requires a positive attitude and a willingness to work together. It means being optimistic and looking for solutions, instead of dwelling on problems. It means being willing to support each other and help each other grow, and it means being committed to the relationship and working together to make it a success.

In short, showing a girl that you are a good team player and can work well in a relationship is crucial for attracting her and falling in love. It demonstrates that you are cooperative, flexible, and willing to work together to achieve common goals. It also shows that you are a good communicator, supportive, and committed to the relationship, which are all important qualities in a romantic partner.

CHAPTER TWENTY-THREE

GOOD LISTENER AND CAN UNDERSTAND HER PERSPECTIVE

Showing a girl that you are a good listener and can understand her perspective is one of the key ways for a boy to attract and fall in love with her. Listening is a fundamental aspect of communication, and it is one of the most important ways to show someone that you care about them and value their thoughts and feelings.

Being a good listener means being present and attentive during conversations. It means putting aside distractions and focusing on the conversation, avoiding interruptions and being fully engaged in what the girl is saying. It also means asking questions, providing feedback, and showing that you are actively listening and paying attention to what she is saying.

In addition to actively listening, understanding her perspective is also crucial. This means trying to see things from her point of view and trying to understand her thoughts and feelings. When you understand her perspective, you can build a deeper connection and bond with her, as you are able to appreciate and understand her experiences and emotions.

Another way to show that you are a good listener and can understand her perspective is to listen without judgment. Avoid making negative comments or criticizing her thoughts and feelings. Instead, be supportive and understanding, and offer words of encouragement. This helps to create a safe and comfortable space where she feels comfortable sharing her thoughts and feelings with you.

Additionally, being a good listener also means being responsive to her needs and being there for her when she needs it. It means being her rock, her confidant, and her biggest supporter. When she knows that she can rely on you and that you are there for her, it builds trust and strengthens the emotional connection between you two.

In short, being a good listener and understanding her perspective is crucial for attracting and falling in love with a girl. It shows that you care about her and value her thoughts and feelings. It also demonstrates that you are trustworthy and dependable, which are important qualities in a romantic partner. Additionally, it lays the foundation for strong and healthy communication, which is crucial for any lasting relationship.

So, if you want to fall in love with a girl, make sure to show her that you are a good listener and can understand her perspective. This will help you to build a deeper connection with her, demonstrate that you care about her and that you are dependable, and lay the foundation for a strong and healthy relationship.

CHAPTER TWENTY-FOUR

RESPONSIBLE AND MATURE PERSON

Showing that you are a responsible and mature person is crucial for attracting a girl and falling in love. Responsibility and maturity are important traits that demonstrate that you are dependable and capable of handling the challenges of a relationship.

Being responsible means being accountable for your actions and being able to follow through on your commitments. It means being reliable and dependable, and it means taking responsibility for your mistakes and making amends when necessary. This shows that you are trustworthy and that you are capable of handling the responsibilities of a relationship.

Maturity, on the other hand, means being able to handle difficult situations and emotions in a mature and controlled manner. It means being able to communicate effectively and resolve conflicts in a healthy and productive way. It also means being able to manage your emotions and being emotionally stable, which are important qualities in a romantic partner.

When you show that you are a responsible and mature person, it demonstrates that you are capable of handling the challenges of a relationship and that you are serious about making it work. It also shows that you are capable of handling the responsibilities and expectations that come with being in a relationship, such as being there for each other, being committed, and being supportive.

Additionally, being responsible and mature also means being able to take care of yourself and your life. This means being able to manage your finances, having a stable job, and having a good support system. It also means being able to make responsible decisions and being able to handle the consequences of your actions.

In short, showing that you are a responsible and mature person is crucial for attracting a girl and falling in love. It demonstrates that you are dependable, trustworthy, and capable of handling the challenges of a relationship. It also shows that you are serious about making it work and that you are capable of handling the responsibilities and expectations that come with being in a relationship. Additionally, it demonstrates that you are capable of taking care of yourself and your life, which are important qualities in a romantic partner.

CHAPTER TWENTY-FIVE

HEALTHY AND BALANCED LIFESTYLE

Having a healthy and balanced lifestyle is important for attracting a girl and falling in love. A healthy lifestyle includes having a balanced diet, regular exercise, and engaging in activities that promote mental and emotional well-being. It also involves managing stress, getting adequate sleep, and maintaining healthy relationships with friends and family.

Showing a girl that you have a healthy and balanced lifestyle can be attractive to her because it demonstrates that you are responsible, self-aware, and take care of yourself. A healthy lifestyle also shows that you are proactive about your well-being and that you are committed to living a fulfilling and meaningful life.

In order to show a girl that you have a healthy and balanced lifestyle, it is important to prioritize your well-being and to make it a part of your daily routine. This could include making time for regular exercise, eating a balanced diet, and engaging in activities that bring you joy and relaxation. Additionally, it is important to manage stress, get enough sleep, and maintain healthy relationships with friends and family.

Having a healthy and balanced lifestyle can also impact your overall confidence and self-esteem. When you take care of yourself and prioritize your well-being, you can feel more confident, energized, and ready to tackle the challenges that come your way. This positive outlook can be attractive to a girl, as confidence and self-assurance are attractive qualities in a partner.

Furthermore, a healthy and balanced lifestyle can also improve your physical and mental health. This can lead to increased energy and focus, which can be beneficial for building a strong and meaningful relationship. Additionally, having a healthy lifestyle can also contribute to longevity and a higher quality of life, which can be important for a long-lasting and fulfilling relationship.

In conclusion, having a healthy and balanced lifestyle is essential for attracting a girl and falling in love. It demonstrates that you are responsible, self-aware, and committed to your well-being. It can also impact your confidence and self-esteem, as well as your overall physical and mental health. By prioritizing your well-being and making it a part of your daily routine, you can show a girl that you have a healthy and balanced lifestyle and that you are ready for a meaningful and lasting relationship.

CHAPTER TWENTY-SIX

POSITIVE AND OPTIMISTIC OUTLOOK ON LIFE

Having a positive and optimistic outlook on life is a critical trait for attracting a girl and falling in love. A positive attitude can bring light into a person's life and make them feel good about themselves and their surroundings. When a boy has a positive and optimistic outlook on life, it can be contagious and can bring happiness to the people around him, including the girl he is trying to fall in love with.

Showing a girl that you have a positive and optimistic outlook on life can demonstrate your confidence and resilience. It shows that you are able to handle challenges and difficulties in a constructive and optimistic way, and that you believe in the power of positive thinking. This can make a girl feel confident and secure around you and can help build a strong emotional connection.

Additionally, having a positive and optimistic outlook on life can help improve the quality of a relationship. When both partners have a positive attitude, they are more likely to work together to overcome challenges and difficulties, and they are more likely to find joy and happiness in their relationship. It can also help create a positive and supportive environment, where both partners can grow and thrive together.

It's important to note that having a positive and optimistic outlook on life is not about ignoring or denying negative situations and emotions. Rather, it's about embracing and accepting them, and focusing on finding solutions and looking for the good in difficult situations.

- To show a girl that you have a positive and optimistic outlook on life, you can practice the following:
- Practice gratitude and appreciate the good things in your life.
- Focus on solutions instead of problems.
- Surround yourself with positive people and activities.
- Cultivate a growth mindset and embrace challenges as opportunities for growth and improvement.
- Avoid complaining and negative thinking.
- Keep a positive attitude, even in difficult situations.
- Embrace change and be open to new experiences.

In conclusion, showing a girl that you have a positive and optimistic outlook on life is a critical step in attracting her and falling in love. A positive attitude can bring happiness, confidence, and security to a relationship, and it can help create a supportive and positive environment where both partners can grow and thrive. By practicing gratitude, focusing on solutions, and embracing change, you can show a girl that you have a positive and optimistic outlook on life and build a strong and lasting relationship.

CHAPTER TWENTY-SEVEN

WILLING TO COMPROMISE AND WORK THROUGH CHALLENGES

Compromise and working through challenges are key components of any successful and healthy relationship. They demonstrate a willingness to put in effort and work towards a common goal, and they show that both partners are committed to making the relationship work. This is why showing a girl that you are willing to compromise and work through challenges is an important step in attracting her and falling in love.

When you are willing to compromise, it shows that you are flexible and open-minded, and that you are willing to consider and respect her perspectives and needs. It also means being willing to make changes and adjustments to accommodate each other, and it means being willing to put aside your own interests and desires for the good of the relationship.

Working through challenges is another important aspect of relationship building. All relationships face challenges and obstacles, and it is how you handle them that can make or break the relationship. When you show a girl that you are willing to work through challenges with her, it demonstrates your commitment and dedication to the relationship. It also shows that you are a problem-solver and that you are willing to put in effort to make things work.

Additionally, working through challenges together can also bring you closer as a couple. It allows you to build trust, communication skills, and a deeper emotional connection. It also helps you grow as individuals and as a couple, and it can lead to a stronger and more fulfilling relationship.

In short, showing a girl that you are willing to compromise and work through challenges is an important step in attracting her and falling in love. It demonstrates your commitment and dedication to the relationship, and it shows that you are willing to put in effort to make things work. Additionally, it builds trust, communication skills, and a deeper emotional connection, which are all essential for a successful and healthy relationship.

CHAPTER TWENTY-EIGHT

WILLING TO GROW AND EVOLVE AS A PERSON

Showing that you are willing to grow and evolve as a person is a key factor in attracting a girl and falling in love. Being open to change and personal growth demonstrates that you are self-aware and committed to being the best version of yourself. It shows that you are not content with remaining stagnant, and that you are willing to work on yourself and make positive changes for the better.

Being willing to grow and evolve also means being open to feedback and criticism. It means being willing to listen to what others have to say about you and using that information to improve yourself. It also means being humble and recognizing that you don't know everything, and that there is always room for growth and improvement.

Additionally, being willing to grow and evolve also means being willing to try new things and take risks. It means being open to new experiences and stepping out of your comfort zone. This not only shows that you are willing to grow, but it also demonstrates that you are adventurous and spontaneous, which can be attractive qualities in a partner.

When a girl sees that you are willing to grow and evolve as a person, it shows that you are committed to your own personal growth and that you are willing to work on yourself. It also demonstrates that you are open-minded and flexible, which can be important qualities in a relationship.

Moreover, being willing to grow and evolve also means being willing to change for the better. It means being willing to make changes in your life and habits in order to be a better person and to improve your relationships. This can include things like working on communication skills, developing empathy, and becoming more self-aware.

In conclusion, showing that you are willing to grow and evolve as a person is an essential factor in attracting a girl and falling in love. It demonstrates that you are self-aware, committed to personal growth, open-minded, and flexible, which are all important qualities in a romantic partner. Additionally, it lays the foundation for a healthy and dynamic relationship, where both partners are constantly working to improve themselves and grow together.

CHAPTER TWENTY-NINE

OPEN TO LEARNING AND SELF-IMPROVEMENT

Showing a girl that you are open to learning and self-improvement is an important factor in attracting her and falling in love. This means being willing to try new things, to expand your knowledge, and to challenge yourself. It also means being open to feedback and being willing to learn from your mistakes.

Self-improvement is a continuous process, and it is a demonstration of your dedication to becoming the best version of yourself. This not only benefits you, but it also makes you a more attractive and desirable partner. When you are open to learning and self-improvement, it shows that you are proactive and driven, and that you are willing to work hard to achieve your goals.

Additionally, being open to learning and self-improvement can help you connect with your partner on a deeper level. When you share your interests, passions, and goals, you can find common ground and have meaningful conversations. It also provides opportunities for shared experiences and activities, which can strengthen your bond.

When you show a girl that you are open to learning and self-improvement, it demonstrates that you are committed to personal growth and that you are willing to put in the effort to become the best version of yourself. This can inspire her to do the same and can lead to a mutually supportive and fulfilling relationship.

However, it is important to note that self-improvement should not be done to impress someone else, but rather to become the best version of yourself. When you are genuine and authentic in your quest for self-improvement, it will show and it will attract others who are also looking for genuine and authentic relationships.

In conclusion, showing a girl that you are open to learning and self-improvement is an important factor in attracting her and falling in love. It demonstrates your dedication to personal growth, your commitment to being the best version of yourself, and your willingness to put in the effort to achieve your goals. When you are open to learning and self-improvement, you can connect with your partner on a deeper level and build a mutually supportive and fulfilling relationship.

CHAPTER THIRTY

GOOD SOCIAL SKILLS AND CAN CONNECT WITH PEOPLE

Good social skills are an essential quality for attracting a girl and falling in love. Being able to connect with people and communicate effectively is a key factor in building strong relationships, and it can make a big difference in how a girl perceives you.

When you have good social skills, you are able to engage in conversations, make people feel comfortable, and build rapport with those around you. This can make you appear confident, friendly, and approachable, which are all attractive qualities in a potential partner. Additionally, having good social skills can help you establish a connection with a girl and get to know her better, which is an important step in building a relationship.

One of the most important aspects of good social skills is effective communication. This means being able to articulate your thoughts and feelings clearly and listen actively to what others have to say. It also means being able to read social cues and respond appropriately, and being able to navigate conversations with ease.

Another important aspect of good social skills is being able to connect with people on a deeper level. This means being able to identify common interests, find common ground, and engage in meaningful conversations. It also means being able to build trust and establish a rapport with others, which is essential for building strong relationships.

Having good social skills can also make you a better listener, and can help you understand and empathize with others. This means being able to put yourself in someone else's shoes and understand their perspective, which is an important aspect of building strong relationships.

In short, having good social skills is a key factor in attracting a girl and falling in love. Being able to connect with people and communicate effectively can make you appear confident, friendly, and approachable, and can help you establish a connection with a girl and get to know her better. Additionally, being a good listener and understanding others is an important aspect of building strong relationships, and it can be achieved through good social skills.

CHAPTER THIRTY-ONE

WIDE RANGE OF INTERESTS AND HOBBIES

Showing a girl that you have a wide range of interests and hobbies is a crucial aspect of attracting her and falling in love. When a boy has a range of interests and hobbies, it demonstrates that he is well-rounded, curious, and passionate about life. These qualities are incredibly attractive and can make a girl feel drawn to him.

Having a range of interests and hobbies also shows that you are open-minded and willing to try new things. This can be especially appealing to a girl who is looking for someone who is not afraid to step out of their comfort zone and experience new things with her.

In addition to being attractive, having a range of interests and hobbies also helps to keep the relationship fresh and interesting. When both partners have a range of interests, it provides a variety of topics to talk about and a never-ending list of activities to do together. This helps to keep the relationship engaging and dynamic, which is important for maintaining a strong connection.

Moreover, when a boy has a range of interests and hobbies, it shows that he has a sense of purpose and direction in life. This can make a girl feel secure in the relationship, knowing that he is focused and driven.

It's important to note that having a range of interests and hobbies does not mean that you have to be an expert in everything. It simply means that you are interested in exploring new things and have a passion for life. This can be as simple as trying a new hobby, reading a new book, or exploring a new city.

In conclusion, showing a girl that you have a wide range of interests and hobbies is a key aspect of attracting her and falling in love. It demonstrates that you are well-rounded, curious, and passionate about life, which are incredibly attractive qualities. Additionally, having a range of interests and hobbies helps to keep the relationship fresh, interesting, and dynamic, which is important for maintaining a strong connection. So, embrace your interests and hobbies and let them be a part of who you are.

CHAPTER THIRTY-TWO

HEALTHY SENSE OF SELF-WORTH AND SELF-ESTEEM

Having a healthy sense of self-worth and self-esteem is crucial for attracting a girl and falling in love. When a boy has a positive view of himself, he exudes confidence and self-assuredness, which can be incredibly attractive to a girl. On the other hand, when a boy lacks self-worth and self-esteem, he may come across as insecure or uncertain, which can be a turn-off.

Having self-worth means having a sense of your own value and worth as a person. It means recognizing your strengths and weaknesses and having the confidence to be yourself, even in the face of criticism or rejection. It means believing that you are deserving of love and happiness, and it means being comfortable in your own skin.

Self-esteem, on the other hand, refers to the level of respect and confidence you have in yourself. It means feeling good about yourself and your abilities, and it means accepting and loving yourself, even in the face of flaws and imperfections.

When a boy has a healthy sense of self-worth and self-esteem, he demonstrates that he is comfortable with himself and confident in his abilities. This can make him more attractive to a girl, as she will sense that he is secure in who he is and is not easily influenced by the opinions of others. Additionally, a boy with a healthy sense of self-worth and self-esteem is less likely to be overly-needy or clingy in a relationship, which can be a turn-off for many girls.

However, it is important to note that having a healthy sense of self-worth and self-esteem does not mean being arrogant or entitled. It means being confident in yourself, but also being humble and respectful of others. It means recognizing that everyone has their own strengths and weaknesses, and it means being kind and understanding of those around you.

In short, having a healthy sense of self-worth and self-esteem is essential for attracting a girl and falling in love. It demonstrates that you are confident in yourself and comfortable in your own skin, and it lays the foundation for a healthy and fulfilling relationship. By working on your self-worth and self-esteem, you can become the best version of yourself, and you can attract the girl of your dreams.

CHAPTER THIRTY-THREE

GOOD SELF-CONTROL AND CAN MANAGE YOUR EMOTIONS

Showing a girl that you have good self-control and can manage your emotions is crucial for attracting her and falling in love. Self-control and emotional management are important qualities that demonstrate maturity, stability, and responsibility. They are also key indicators of the ability to handle conflict and stress, which are important aspects of any relationship.

Self-control refers to the ability to regulate your actions, thoughts, and emotions in response to a situation. It means being able to resist impulsive or reactive behaviors and instead making conscious, thoughtful decisions. When a boy demonstrates self-control, it shows that he is in control of himself and his emotions and that he is capable of making rational decisions, even in difficult situations.

Emotional management refers to the ability to regulate and control your emotions, particularly in response to stress or conflict. It means being able to stay calm and composed, even in challenging situations, and being able to manage your emotions in a healthy and productive way. When a boy demonstrates emotional management, it shows that he is capable of handling stress and conflict in a healthy way, which is important for the health and longevity of any relationship.

When a girl sees that a boy has good self-control and emotional management, she is more likely to trust him and feel comfortable with him. It shows that he is capable of handling difficult situations in a mature and responsible way, which is important for building trust and emotional connection. Additionally, it also demonstrates that he is responsible, dependable, and capable of managing his emotions, which are important qualities in a romantic partner.

However, it is important to note that demonstrating self-control and emotional management is not just about suppressing or hiding your emotions. It means being able to express your emotions in a healthy and productive way, and it means being able to communicate your needs and feelings in a respectful and considerate way.

To show a girl that you have good self-control and emotional management, you can practice mindfulness and self-reflection. This means taking the time to reflect on your thoughts and emotions and being conscious of how you respond to situations. You can also practice active listening and communication skills, which can help you manage your emotions in a healthy way and communicate your needs and feelings effectively.

In short, showing a girl that you have good self-control and can manage your emotions is crucial for attracting her and falling in love. It demonstrates maturity, stability, and responsibility, and it lays the foundation for trust and emotional connection. However, it is important to remember that demonstrating self-control and emotional management also means being able to express your emotions in a healthy and productive way and communicating your needs and feelings effectively.

CHAPTER THIRTY-FOUR

GOOD SELF-AWARENESS AND UNDERSTANDING OF YOUR OWN EMOTIONS

Showing good self-awareness and understanding of one's own emotions is a crucial aspect of attracting a girl and falling in love. Self-awareness refers to the ability to recognize and understand one's own emotions, thoughts, and behaviors. It is the foundation of emotional intelligence and is essential for building healthy relationships.

When a boy has good self-awareness, he is able to understand his own emotions and thoughts, and he is better equipped to regulate them. This means that he can identify when he is feeling upset or frustrated, for example, and he can find healthy ways to manage these emotions. As a result, he is less likely to react impulsively or lash out in anger, which can be damaging to a relationship.

Additionally, good self-awareness allows a boy to understand why he feels the way he does and to communicate his emotions effectively. This means that he can explain why he is feeling upset or hurt, for example, and he can do so in a way that is calm and respectful. This can be incredibly important in resolving conflicts and building trust and understanding in a relationship.

In order to show a girl that you have good self-awareness and understanding of your own emotions, it is important to practice self-reflection and introspection. This means taking the time to reflect on your emotions and thoughts, and it means being honest with yourself about why you feel the way you do.

Another way to show good self-awareness is by being open and honest about your emotions with your partner. This means not being afraid to express your feelings and being willing to listen to hers. It also means being willing to compromise and find solutions that work for both of you.

It is also important to show empathy and understanding towards your partner's emotions. This means being able to put yourself in her shoes and understand why she may be feeling upset or hurt. It also means being willing to listen to her and to provide comfort and support when she needs it.

Furthermore, being able to manage your own emotions and not letting them control you is a sign of good self-awareness. This means being able to take a step back and assess a situation objectively, rather than reacting impulsively. It also means being able to manage stress and anxiety, and finding healthy ways to cope with difficult emotions.

In conclusion, showing good self-awareness and understanding of your own emotions is crucial for attracting a girl and falling in love. It is the foundation of emotional intelligence and is essential for building healthy relationships. It involves being able to understand and regulate your own emotions, being open and honest about your feelings, showing empathy and understanding towards your partner's emotions, and being able to manage your own emotions effectively. By demonstrating good self-awareness, you can build trust, understanding, and a strong emotional connection with a girl, which are key ingredients for a successful and lasting relationship.

CHAPTER THIRTY-FIVE

Sense of Responsibility and Commitment

Having a sense of responsibility and commitment is a crucial aspect of attracting a girl and falling in love. When a boy shows that he is responsible and committed, it demonstrates that he is reliable, dependable, and trustworthy. It also shows that he is serious about his relationships and that he is willing to make a long-term commitment.

Being responsible means that a boy takes his obligations and duties seriously and follows through on his commitments. It means being accountable for his actions and decisions and being willing to make changes when necessary. When a boy shows that he is responsible, it demonstrates that he is mature and capable of handling important tasks and responsibilities, which can be attractive to a girl.

Commitment, on the other hand, means being dedicated and devoted to a relationship and working towards making it last. It means being willing to make sacrifices and compromises for the sake of the relationship and being committed to the idea of building a future together. When a boy shows that he is committed, it demonstrates that he is serious about the relationship and that he is willing to put in the time and effort to make it work.

Having a sense of responsibility and commitment also means being supportive and understanding towards the girl. It means being there for her when she needs it, both emotionally and physically, and being willing to help her when she needs it. It also means being non-judgmental and open-minded, and it means encouraging her to be true to herself.

In addition to attracting a girl, having a sense of responsibility and commitment is also important for building a healthy and lasting relationship. When a boy is responsible and committed, it demonstrates that he is willing to invest in the relationship and make it a priority. It also shows that he is trustworthy and dependable, which are important qualities in a romantic partner. Additionally, it lays the foundation for acceptance and understanding, which are crucial for any healthy and lasting relationship.

However, it is important to note that having a sense of responsibility and commitment does not mean that a boy should sacrifice his own wants and needs for the sake of the relationship. It means finding a balance between his own needs and the needs of the relationship and working together towards a common goal.

In conclusion, showing a girl that you have a sense of responsibility and commitment is essential for attracting her and falling in love. It demonstrates that you are reliable, dependable, and trustworthy, and that you are serious about the relationship and willing to invest in making it last. Additionally, it lays the foundation for a healthy and lasting relationship, based on trust, respect, and understanding. By demonstrating your responsibility and commitment, you will not only attract a girl, but you will also create a strong and lasting connection that will endure for years to come.

CHAPTER THIRTY-SIX

STRONG SENSE OF SELF AND PERSONAL IDENTITY

Having a strong sense of self and personal identity is crucial for attracting a girl and falling in love. It means knowing who you are, what you stand for, and what you want in life. It means having a clear understanding of your values, beliefs, and goals, and it means being comfortable in your own skin.

Having a strong sense of self and personal identity also means being confident in your abilities and decisions. It means being able to make choices that align with your values and beliefs, even when they may not be popular or easy. It means being able to stand up for yourself and what you believe in, and it means being resilient in the face of challenges and setbacks.

When a boy has a strong sense of self and personal identity, it shows that he is secure and confident in who he is. It also demonstrates that he is mature and has a clear direction in life, which can be incredibly attractive to a girl. Additionally, it lays the foundation for a healthy and balanced relationship, as it means that the boy is less likely to be swayed by outside influences or to compromise his own values and beliefs.

However, developing a strong sense of self and personal identity takes time and effort. It involves exploring your interests, values, and beliefs, and it means being honest with yourself about what is truly important to you. It also means being open to new experiences and perspectives, and it means embracing change and growth.

Having a strong sense of self and personal identity can also be challenging, as it means being vulnerable and opening yourself up to the possibility of rejection or criticism. However, the rewards of having a clear understanding of who you are and what you stand for are well worth the effort.

When it comes to attracting a girl and falling in love, being authentic and genuine is key. It means being yourself, rather than trying to be someone you're not. It means embracing your strengths and weaknesses, and it means being honest about your feelings and intentions.

In addition to being authentic and genuine, it is also important to show a strong sense of self and personal identity. This means having confidence in yourself and your abilities, and it means being comfortable in your own skin. It also means being ambitious and having goals in life, and it means being respectful and considerate of her feelings.

In short, having a strong sense of self and personal identity is essential for attracting a girl and falling in love. It demonstrates confidence, maturity, and direction, and it lays the foundation for a healthy and balanced relationship. By being authentic and genuine, and by embracing your strengths and weaknesses, you can show a girl that you are someone she can trust and depend on.

CHAPTER THIRTY-SEVEN

HAVE A SENSE OF SELF-RESPECT AND SELF-LOVE

Showing a sense of self-respect and self-love is essential for attracting a girl and falling in love. This not only makes you a more confident and attractive person, but it also demonstrates that you are someone who is emotionally healthy and ready for a relationship.

Self-respect means having a high regard for yourself and your own worth. It means having a clear understanding of your values, beliefs, and boundaries and being willing to stand up for them. It also means treating yourself with kindness and compassion, and not settling for anything less than what you deserve.

Self-love means having a positive and accepting attitude towards yourself, even with your flaws and imperfections. It means taking care of yourself physically, emotionally, and mentally, and not relying on someone else to validate your worth.

When you have a sense of self-respect and self-love, it shows that you are in control of your own life and that you are not afraid to be yourself. It also demonstrates that you are confident, assertive, and comfortable in your own skin, which are all attractive qualities to a girl.

Moreover, having a sense of self-respect and self-love also means that you are less likely to compromise your values or to tolerate unhealthy or disrespectful behavior from others. This makes you a more stable and trustworthy partner, which can help to build a stronger and healthier relationship.

In addition to demonstrating self-respect and self-love, it is also important to communicate it to a girl. This means being honest and straightforward about your needs, beliefs, and boundaries, and being willing to stand up for yourself when necessary. It also means being kind and understanding towards yourself, and not being too hard on yourself when things don't go as planned.

To show a sense of self-respect and self-love, it is also important to prioritize your own well-being and to make time for self-care. This could include activities such as exercise, hobbies, and spending time with friends and family. By taking care of yourself, you show that you value and respect yourself, and that you are not willing to compromise your own happiness for someone else.

In short, showing a sense of self-respect and self-love is essential for attracting a girl and falling in love. It demonstrates that you are confident, assertive, and comfortable in your own skin, and that you are emotionally healthy and ready for a relationship. Additionally, by taking care of yourself and being honest and straightforward about your needs and beliefs, you can build a strong and healthy relationship based on mutual respect and understanding

CHAPTER THIRTY-EIGHT

OPEN TO DIFFERENT CULTURES, BACKGROUNDS AND WAYS OF LIFE

Showing an open mind and a willingness to embrace different cultures, backgrounds, and ways of life is an important aspect of attracting a girl and falling in love. The world is full of diverse and unique individuals, and being open to these differences is a key component of building strong and meaningful relationships.

Having an open mind means being willing to learn about and understand different cultures, backgrounds, and ways of life. This includes being curious about new experiences and seeking out new perspectives. It means being accepting of different beliefs, traditions, and values, even if they are different from your own.

Being open to different cultures and backgrounds also means being tolerant and respectful of others. This means avoiding judgment or discrimination based on differences and instead, embracing the richness and diversity of the world.

In addition to these benefits, embracing diversity can also be an exciting and enriching experience. When you are open to different cultures and ways of life, you have the opportunity to learn new things and expand your horizons. This can lead to personal growth and a deeper understanding of the world around you.

When you show a girl that you are open to different cultures and backgrounds, it demonstrates that you are a compassionate and empathetic individual. This can be very attractive to a girl, as it shows that you are interested in her and that you are willing to understand her perspective.

It also shows that you are a good listener and that you are interested in getting to know her. When you take the time to listen to a girl and understand her background and experiences, it can help to build a deeper connection and a sense of trust.

Moreover, being open to different cultures and ways of life can also make you a more interesting and well-rounded individual. This can be especially attractive to a girl, as it shows that you are curious, adventurous, and that you are willing to explore the world.

In conclusion, showing an open mind and a willingness to embrace different cultures, backgrounds, and ways of life is a key component of attracting a girl and falling in love. It demonstrates that you are a compassionate and empathetic individual who is interested in getting to know her and understanding her perspective. It also shows that you are a good listener and that you are willing to learn and grow. By embracing diversity, you can expand your horizons, build strong connections, and experience personal growth, which are all important aspects of any healthy and lasting relationship.

CHAPTER THIRTY-NINE

SENSE OF RESPECT FOR OTHERS

Having a sense of respect for others is an important quality to have in any relationship, and especially when trying to attract and fall in love with a girl. Respect means treating others with dignity and consideration, and it is an essential aspect of any healthy and lasting relationship.

When a boy shows a girl that he has a sense of respect for others, it shows that he is a kind and compassionate person. It also demonstrates that he is mature and responsible, and that he has a strong moral character. These are all important qualities that are attractive to many girls and can help to build a strong emotional connection.

One of the ways to show respect for others is by being polite and courteous. This means using good manners, such as saying "please" and "thank you," and treating others with kindness and understanding. It also means avoiding hurtful or offensive language, and being mindful of the way that your words and actions can affect others.

Another way to show respect for others is by being empathetic and understanding. This means being able to put yourself in someone else's shoes and seeing things from their perspective. It also means being able to listen actively and respond to others in a compassionate and understanding way. When a boy is able to show empathy and understanding, it shows that he is a good communicator and that he is able to connect with others on an emotional level.

Respect also means being considerate of others‘ feelings and needs. This means being willing to compromise and put the needs of others before your own. It also means being able to accept and learn from feedback, and being willing to apologize when you have done something wrong. When a boy is considerate of others’ feelings and needs, it shows that he is selfless and that he is able to put the needs of others before his own.

Finally, respect means being respectful of others‘ boundaries and personal space. This means respecting someone’s decision to say "no" and avoiding coercion or manipulation. It also means being mindful of others’ physical and emotional well-being and avoiding behaviors that can cause harm.

In conclusion, having a sense of respect for others is an important quality to have when trying to attract and fall in love with a girl. It shows that you are a kind, compassionate, and responsible person, and that you have strong moral character. It also demonstrates that you are a good communicator, empathetic, considerate, and respectful of others' boundaries and personal space. All of these qualities are attractive to many girls and can help to build a strong and lasting relationship.

CHAPTER FORTY

Positive Attitude and Energy

Having a positive attitude and energy is crucial for attracting a girl and falling in love. A positive attitude and energy can be contagious, and it can bring joy and happiness into a person's life. It can also help to improve communication and build stronger connections with others.

When you have a positive attitude, you approach life and relationships with optimism and a can-do spirit. You see the good in situations, and you are able to find solutions instead of dwelling on problems. This can make you an attractive and desirable partner because you bring positivity and energy to the relationship.

Additionally, having a positive attitude and energy also means being enthusiastic and energetic. When you are excited and passionate about life, it can be infectious and it can inspire others. It also shows that you are confident and self-assured, which are important qualities in a romantic partner.

One of the best ways to show a girl that you have a positive attitude and energy is to smile and be friendly. Smiling is a universal language of happiness and positivity, and it can help to put others at ease and make them feel comfortable. Additionally, being friendly and approachable can help to break the ice and create an environment of openness and trust.

Another way to show a girl that you have a positive attitude and energy is to focus on the things that bring you joy and happiness. When you are engaged in activities that you enjoy and that make you happy, it shows that you are content and fulfilled. This can be attractive to a girl because it demonstrates that you are in a good place emotionally and that you have a positive outlook on life.

Additionally, having a positive attitude and energy also means being open and receptive to new experiences and ideas. When you are willing to try new things and explore new possibilities, it shows that you are adventurous and spontaneous. This can be attractive to a girl because it demonstrates that you are open-minded and willing to take risks.

Finally, having a positive attitude and energy also means being grateful and appreciative. When you are thankful for what you have, it demonstrates that you are content and satisfied with your life. This can be attractive to a girl because it shows that you are at peace with yourself and that you have a healthy and positive outlook on life.

In conclusion, having a positive attitude and energy is essential for attracting a girl and falling in love. It shows that you are confident, self-assured, and optimistic. It also demonstrates that you are friendly, approachable, and open-minded. Additionally, it lays the foundation for a positive and fulfilling relationship, and it helps to create an environment of trust and happiness. So, make sure to cultivate a positive attitude and energy, and you will be well on your way to attracting the girl of your dreams.

CHAPTER FORTY-ONE

GOOD LISTENER AND CAN EMPATHIZE WITH HER FEELINGS

Showing a girl that you are a good listener and can empathize with her feelings is a crucial aspect of attracting her and falling in love. Being a good listener is not just about hearing what she has to say, but actively engaging in the conversation and demonstrating that you care about her thoughts and feelings. Empathy, on the other hand, means being able to understand and share her emotions, which is a key component of building a strong emotional connection.

Good listening skills are essential for any relationship. When you actively listen to a girl, it shows that you value her and that you are willing to take the time to understand her perspective. It also demonstrates that you are respectful and considerate of her feelings, which is important in building trust and emotional connection.

Empathy is also a critical component in any relationship. When you are empathetic, you are able to understand and share her emotions, which can make her feel heard and understood. This is especially important when she is going through a difficult time or is feeling overwhelmed, as it can help to provide comfort and support.

In order to show a girl that you are a good listener and can empathize with her feelings, there are several key things you can do. First, it is important to actively engage in the conversation and demonstrate that you are paying attention. This means asking questions, providing feedback, and avoiding distractions, such as checking your phone or being preoccupied with other things.

Second, it is important to be responsive and understanding. This means being able to identify and respond to her emotions, and being willing to put yourself in her shoes. It also means being non-judgmental and open-minded, and avoiding criticism or negativity.

Finally, it is important to be patient and persistent. Good listening and empathy are skills that can be developed over time, and it is important to be patient and persistent in your efforts to improve. This means taking the time to really listen and understand her perspective, and being willing to make changes to your own behavior if necessary.

In conclusion, showing a girl that you are a good listener and can empathize with her feelings is crucial for attracting her and falling in love. It demonstrates that you value and care about her, and it lays the foundation for strong and healthy communication, which is important in any lasting relationship. Whether you are just starting to get to know a girl, or you have been together for a while, making a conscious effort to be a good listener and to demonstrate empathy can help to deepen your connection and strengthen your relationship.

CHAPTER FORTY-TWO

CONCLUSION

In conclusion, attracting a girl and making her fall in love with you is a combination of several important factors, including confidence, genuineness, interest in getting to know her, ambition, respect, being a good listener, support, and belief.

Confidence is key when it comes to attracting a girl. It is important to be confident in yourself and your abilities and to present yourself in a positive and attractive way.

Being genuine and authentic is also crucial. Don't try to be someone you're not, as it is important to be true to yourself and to show the girl who you really are. This will help her see the real you and form a genuine connection.

Showing interest in getting to know her and actively listening to her is also important. Ask questions, be engaged in the conversation, and demonstrate that you value her thoughts and feelings.

Having ambition and goals in life is also attractive to girls. It shows that you have a sense of purpose and drive, and it can help her see you as a reliable and dependable partner.

Respect and consideration for her feelings is also crucial. Treat her with kindness and understanding, and be mindful of her emotions.

Being a good listener and demonstrating that you care about what she has to say is also essential. This can help her feel heard and understood and can lay the foundation for strong and healthy communication.

Finally, being supportive and believing in her is also important. Be her cheerleader, have faith in her abilities, and be there for her when she needs you.

In short, attracting a girl and making her fall in love with you requires a combination of several important qualities, including confidence, genuineness, interest, ambition, respect, being a good listener, support, and belief. By demonstrating these qualities, you can increase your chances of attracting a girl and forming a lasting and meaningful connection.

9 798889 592440

Printed by Libri Plureos GmbH in Hamburg,
Germany